A GLASS FACE
IN THE RAIN

Also by William Stafford

Stories That Could Be True
Someday, Maybe
Allegiances
The Rescued Year
Traveling Through the Dark
West of Your City

A GLASS FACE
IN THE RAIN

· NEW POEMS ·

WILLIAM STAFFORD

1817

HARPER & ROW, PUBLISHERS, New York
Cambridge, Philadelphia, San Francisco, London
Mexico City, São Paulo, Sydney

Copyright acknowledgments appear on page 125.

A GLASS FACE IN THE RAIN. Copyright © 1982 by William Stafford. All rights reserved. Printed in the United States of America. No part of this book may be used or reproduced in any manner whatsoever without written permission except in the case of brief quotations embodied in critical articles and reviews. For information address Harper & Row. Publishers, Inc., 10 East 53rd Street, New York, N.Y. 10022. Published simultaneously in Canada by Fitzhenry & Whiteside Limited, Toronto.

FIRST EDITION

Designer: Abigail Sturges

Library of Congress Cataloging in Publication Data

Stafford, William Edgar, 1914–
 A glass face in the rain.

 I. Title.
PS3537.T143G5   1982   811'.54   82-47534
                                     AACR2

ISBN 0-06-015046-7   82 83 84 85 86 10 9 8 7 6 5 4 3 2 1
ISBN 0-06-090983-8 (pbk.) 82 83 84 85 86 10 9 8 7 6 5 4 3 2 1

CONTENTS

Smoke Signals—a Dedication 11

PART ONE
A TOUCH ON YOUR SLEEVE

How It Began 13

Tuned in Late One Night 15
Friends 16
Rover 17
Knowing 18
They Say 19
A Touch on Your Sleeve 20
Glimpses 21
Looking Across the River 22
Our Cave 24
Not Very Loud 25
Why We Need Fantasy 26
Passing a Pile of Stones 27
An Event at Big Eddy 28
How to Get Back 29
Some Night Again 30

PART TWO
THINGS THAT COME

Things That Come 31

There Is Blindness 33
An Old Pickerel in Walden Pond 34
Finding Out 35
Acoma Mesa 36
Dark Wind 37
A Glimpse in the Crowd 38
Friends: A Recognition 39
Class Reunion 40
Sabbath 41
A Child's Face in a Small Town 42
Watching a Candle 43
Child in the Evening 44
Murder Bridge 45
Seeing and Perceiving 46
Maybe 47
How It Is 48
A Late Guest 49
Later 50
In a Corner 51
Why I Say Adios 52
Remembering 53

PART THREE
REVELATIONS

Sending These Messages 55

A Glass Face in the Rain 57
Yellow Cars 58
Torque 59
My Life 60

A Message from Space   61
Revelation   62
On the Road Last Night   63
After Arguing Against the Contention
    That Art Must Come from Discontent   64
A Course in Creative Writing   65
Things I Learned Last Week   66
Incident   67
Fiction   68
Our Kind   69
Hanging Tough   70
Learning to Like the New School   71
A Catechism   72
School Days   73
We Interrupt to Bring You   74
My Mother Was a Soldier   75
Anticipating   76
When You Go Anywhere   77

PART FOUR

TROUBLESHOOTING

Now wait—   79

Once in the 40's   81
Around You, Your House   82
A Cameo of Your Mother   83
Ruby Was Her Name   84
At the Falls: A Birthday Picture   85
Letting You Go   86
Troubleshooting   87
A Letter Not to Deliver   88

Having the Right Name   89
A Day to Remember   90
Remembering Brother Bob   91
Places with Meaning   92
Confessor   93
A Scene   94
With Neighbors One Afternoon   95
Absences   96

PART FIVE

THE COLOR THAT REALLY IS

A Tentative Welcome to Readers   97

The Color That Really Is   99
A Journey   100
Friends, Farewell   101
If I Could Be Like Wallace
    Stevens   102
Yellow Flowers   103
Salvaged Parts   104
Survivor   105
One Time   106
Little Night Stories   107
Receiver   108
From Hallmark or Somewhere   109
Much Have I Traveled   110
Once in a Dream   111
The Late Flight   112
What Ever Happened to the Beats?   113
What I'll See That Afternoon   114
Pegleg Lookout   115

Yucca Flowers   116
From Our Balloon over the
    Provinces   117

Index of Titles   119
Index of First Lines   122

Smoke Signals
—a dedication—

*There are people on a parallel way. We do not
see them often, or even think of them often,
but it is precious to us that they are sharing
the world. Something about how they have accepted
their lives, or how the sunlight happens to them,
helps us to hold the strange, enigmatic days
in line for our own living. It is important
that these people know this recognition, but
it is also important that no purpose or obligation
related to this be intruded into their lives.*

*This book intends to be for anyone, but especially
for those on that parallel way: here is a smoke
signal, unmistakable but unobtrusive—we are
following what comes, going through the world,
knowing each other, building our little fires.*

PART ONE

A TOUCH ON YOUR SLEEVE

How It Began

They struggled their legs and blindly loved, those puppies
inside my jacket as I walked through town. They crawled
for warmth and licked each other—their poor mother
dead, and one kind boy to save them. I spread
my arms over their world and hurried along.

At Ellen's place I knocked and waited—the tumult
invading my sleeves, all my jacket alive.
When she came to the door we tumbled—black, white,
gray, hungry—all over the living room floor
together, rolling, whining, happy and blind.

TUNED IN LATE ONE NIGHT

Listen—this is a faint station
left alive in the vast universe.
I was left here to tell you a message
designed for your instruction or comfort,
but now that my world is gone I crave
expression pure as all the space
around me: I want to tell what is. . . .

Remember?—we learned that still-face way,
to wait in election or meeting and then
to choose the side that wins, a leader
that lasted, a president that stayed in?
But some of us knew even then it was better
to lose if that was the way our chosen
side came out, in truth, at the end.

It's like this, truth is: it's looking out while everything
happens; being in a place of your own,
between your ears; and any person
you face will get the full encounter
of your self. When you hear any news
you ought to register delight or pain
depending on where you really live.

Now I am fading, with this ambition:
to read with my brights full on,
to write on a clear glass typewriter,
to listen with sympathy,
to speak like a child.

FRIENDS

How far friends are! They forget you,
most days. They have to, I know; but still,
it's lonely just being far and a friend.
I put my hand out—this chair, this table—
so near: touch, that's how to live.
Call up a friend? All right, but the phone
itself is what loves you, warm on your ear,
on your hand. Or, you lift a pen
to write—it's not that far person
but this familiar pen that comforts.
Near things: Friend, here's my hand.

ROVER

She came out of the field—low
cloud and the land even more dark
where it rolled wide, our farm. She came
limping our gate into the yard
and up to the door. For greeting, I
held out my hand. I felt the tongue touch
my palm, and a breath came: something
entering my whole life in a rush.

What came to me in trust no one
could take away. I knew
it was mine. Not father, even, or mother,
could end the new feeling: *mine.*
Now I belonged wherever dark
flowed, from that night on,
anywhere, any touch that was kind.

KNOWING

To know the other world you turn
your hand the way a bird finds angles
of the wind: what the wing feels
pours off your hand. Things invisible
come true, and you can tell. But are
there shy realities we cannot prove?
Your hand can make the sign—but begs for
more than can be told: even the world
can't dive fast enough to know that other world.

THEY SAY

Now and then in some sound you discover
a different country. Once in a barn
open and empty my guitar jumped
in my hand. Often I went back hunting
what happened, but it was always gone.

When we came down through Canada
playing at stampedes in Chilko, and Babine,
and Charlie Lake, there came a time—the drum
and the weather just so. But in Peace River
it changed and never got that way again.

But there's a country beyond all of those, to be
found and then lost. You cross borders toward home,
smuggling a whole state legally, glancing
aside at the wind or the patrol. They want you
to have it. They say, "Song?" and they let it come.

A TOUCH ON YOUR SLEEVE

Consider the slow descent
that a dandelion puff once found
(a plane had carried it so far away
you couldn't imagine it could come down)—

Afloat in space hardly even air
that wavery journey began—
a slight parachute, no center at all,
a nothing that follows the slightest wind.

"Now where might Earth turn gold?" it says,
"that the Midas touch may not be gone."
(One seed could make a meadow glow:
the slow decisioning descends.)

It comes down mixed with snow, a seed
from far that hitched with wind,
and your sweater sleeve is for landing on
(and you are not doing important things).

That seedflake melts without a trace,
that golden touch, Midas for friend—
but it brushes your sleeve in the right place
and your life becomes important again.

GLIMPSES

One time when the wind blows it is years
from now. I am talking with others and
we are telling all the stories except
that one we are in, then someone starts ours:
the wind stops, we look back and then forward.
The voice carries us on, and we try to be what it says.

There is an embrace on a street corner;
two people greet, and make obsolete all the past.
They research those years for the key
event that separated them, but they can't
find it. They part again, and they never
find what it is they have missed.

Walking along, any time,
I find clues to tomorrow—how hard
a poppy is orange, how alert the leaves
are where the streetlight finds them.
My debt to the world begins again,
that I am part of this permanent dream.

At someone's pretension a thought comes—Saint Augustine:
a morning cloud throws a shadow but the sun
says light. Our time goes on, a spider
spins, the wind examines the ground
for clues—just being is a big enough job,
no time for anything else.

LOOKING ACROSS THE RIVER

We were driving the river road.
It was at night. "There's the island,"
someone said. And we all looked across
at the light where the hermit lived.

"I'd be afraid to live there"—
it was Ken the driver who spoke.
He shivered and let us feel
the fear that made him shake.

Over to that dark island
my thought had already crossed—
I felt the side of the house
and the night wind unwilling to rest.

For the first time in all my life
I became someone else:
it was dark; others were going their way;
the river and I kept ours.

We came on home that night;
the road led us on. Everything
we said was louder—it was hollow,
and sounded dark like a bridge.

Somewhere I had lost someone—
so dear or so great or so fine
that I never cared again: as if
time dimmed, and color and sound were gone.

Come for me now, World—
whatever is near, come close.
I have been over the water
and lived there all alone.

OUR CAVE

Because it was good, we were afraid.
It went down dark, dark. After a
bend it was night. We didn't tell
anybody. All summer it was ours.
I remember best when horses went by
shaking the ground. It was war, we said,
and they wouldn't find us. Once we heard
someone stumbling and crying: we blew out
the candle and waited a long time till quiet.
It came, and the dark was closer than ever.
Now when we close our eyes, we are there
again, anywhere: we hid it well.
We buried in it the best things we had
and covered it over with branches and leaves.

NOT VERY LOUD

Now is the time of the moths that come
in the evening. They are around, just being
there, at windows and doors. They crowd
the lights, planing in from dark fields
and liking it in town. They accept each other
as they fly or crawl. How do they know
what is coming? Their furred flight,
softer than down, announces a quiet
approach under whatever is loud.

What are moths good for? Maybe they offer
something we need, a fluttering
near the edge of our sight, and they may carry
whatever is needed for us to watch
all through those long nights in our still,
vacant houses, if there is another war.

WHY WE NEED FANTASY

It's a sensational story
as it slowly falls, the rain,
or the used-up sunlight all day
onto the dim of the land,
where rivers have to believe.

Followed by that rain
we hunt a cave to hide in,
or we try to be brave, or we find—
by moving fast—the wind
that lurks in the air we breathe.

Some animals find a way
to keep from being found—
they eat the days they live:
that brave, who needs a dream?
But there aren't enough caves, you know—

For animals that have our need.

PASSING A PILE OF STONES

A shadow hides in every stone.
When the sun goes down the shadow crawls
from inside its place; it reaches out.
When we walk by, one part of our step
touches alive the hidden self
awaiting nightfall to be real.

Could there be a light so far that when
you stop you make a shadow forever?

AN EVENT AT BIG EDDY

The whole weight of the river
leans into the rock at Big Eddy.
We camped and let that rush
report something all night to us—
a hint of the earth tied down
quivering like an animal.

Since then it is faces like that,
trying not to act, I see in a crowd:
I watch those knowers wild
when the spill of their lives hits
them and the spin of the earth
blares more than any person can stand.

That stillness comes home,
the way it will some day:
the awful torque at the pole
grab the center of the world, and
everyone run into the street, and know,
and hold the face still with both hands.

HOW TO GET BACK

By believing, you can get there—that edge
the light-years leave behind, where no one
living today survives. You can get there
where the lake turns to stone and your boat
rocks, once, then hangs tilted a long time:
in that instant you don't want to leave,
where talk finds truth, slides near
and away; where music holds its moment
forever, and then forever again.

You are only a wandering dot that fails—
that has already failed, but you can get
there. And you can come back—the boat
moves; talk turns ordinary; music
is hunting its moment again.
Around you people don't know how you
and themselves and the whole world
hover in belief. They've never been gone.

SOME NIGHT AGAIN

When the world vanishes, I will come back
here by the power of my dreams and create it
again, starting where that clear
depth in the mountain lake began,
where you swam one night across the moonlight
and I thought: Still, it's good, though it has to end.

PART TWO

THINGS THAT COME

Things That Come

After it came down from the mountains
the first house the wind found was ours—
tapped and rattled and pushed by curious
little pieces of air, and then shoved and
shaken by the wild-riding storm.

My father looked up—understood: that
voice in the night was tamed. Whatever struck
our house—let it come. He read on,
a story of a wolf and a man, a blizzard
where they warmed each other like friends.

There were other stories he promised he would
tell sometime; and we knew how far
he thought—his old home was blasted
away, and a bigger storm might come. He saved
us, though, that night, by how he cocked his head.

You think my poems are soft? That there isn't
a wolf in them? Listen—through all that swoop
down from the mountains my curious, quiet
breath comes: I am frantic to find these
little stones; I am building a house for us.

THERE IS BLINDNESS

There is blindness; there is
vision: accepting the symptoms
is not helping the victim.

Brought close and loud, faces
remind you—you deserve anger,
even their anger:

Pain is real.
But over their shoulders
there looms real home—

There's the world.

AN OLD PICKEREL IN WALDEN POND

One winter—open, I remember it was—
after the first clear ice this man used to lie
face down staring deeper than anyone else
and making notes in a little book.

His eyes were close, light blue; a scarf
huddled his throat. He seemed to be trying to see
out of a window he was trapped behind.
With longing he searched. The sky looked over his
    shoulder.

One day he did a little dance on the ice,
a shuffling step to make the ice crack, a report
like a gun; then he walked away like an Indian,
measuring where the zigzag line went.

That night the whole ice eye filled up with snow.

FINDING OUT

I am that poor Marie, the sinner, who died in the cave.
　　　　　　　　　—Shadows on the Rock

No, not dark. Even at night a glow from a shaft
spread near me. But hardly a breath, and the sound
only of stones becoming themselves, or denying it.

Now I am seeking the reason my life was in the world:
all up and down these roads I am turning the leaves,
moving the grass, turning on my tongue the secret words.

At the last I will be able to say, "Forgive me,"
and be quiet. Almost saved now, I wander, brought back
by the American woman with the wide hat, the cave-looking
　　eyes.

I will go by now. Think about me, my
story, how I was in the world—
maybe to help you—a long time ago.

ACOMA MESA

Surrounded by air, we live where
a step ends the world. Nothing
begins where we look down. We never
take that other step. A blue wall
holds home together.

You in your home: birds weave
around you too something you
never dare touch. At night you
come in and are near: the world falls,
a long silent plunge through the sky.

DARK WIND

Jean, who no longer is, was
with somebody else. All the air
in the world poured over the lake
that night, warm, and a moon on each
wave as it came. And finally one with a splash
that gasped on the sand, "Save me." I looked
again—it was Jean. I saved her, that once,
who swam back to the dock that night
with somebody else. *I wonder if she got
my letters.* I remember I learned she died,
all the air in the world pouring past.

A GLIMPSE IN THE CROWD

A parachute catches and suddenly you know
you've been falling for years. God slows
it. He can't stop it, but
He can let you look back. Things
in your life begin to wake up: the yard where
sunlight collected, the end of your street
where the world began. You reach out across
a widening place—almost, almost. . . .
Then suddenly you begin falling again.

FRIENDS: A RECOGNITION

It came silent in my thought
that someone else, a friend so dear
they shone, had followed me into
a cave. I was a prisoner of their light,
and felt with my hands along the edge
of the room they made. In me was dark;
the light they brought was—in me—shade.

And it came silent in my thought
how dim I was, and all my life
groped inside my hands to find
one little jewel of light to share:
my habit was the dark, and they
could save, those friends whose faces followed
me and shone forth everywhere.

CLASS REUNION

Where others ran I run my hand
across a photograph. It shows
me standing where I am, applauding them.
They are far along the track; it's
evening, lights coming on. I
didn't mean to win like this. I mean,
they're gone. I mean,
I didn't win.

SABBATH

A light—it's only the sun—has broken
into a church to deliver jewels across
the floor. They roll and wait.
Fallen from heights onto wood
or stone, these cat-footed worshipers
flow among shadows.

If you bow still enough these
jewels from a window come true
all the way down to your feet.
You hear sounds the organ was
almost making when it wandered through
songs back of you, years ago.

It wasn't that the promises would
help, later: it was this—they had
come true before you got there,
and were hiding to come true again
whenever you looked up from prayer.
And those window stories always follow you even
  now—

Down alleys, up marble stairs.

A CHILD'S FACE IN A SMALL TOWN

Sometimes it happens a storm
or fear hits, or sometimes
only days parachuting from a clear sky
into your life. Whatever,
you turn your face calmly
toward what comes: it will pass,
it will pass like the circus on Main Street
while you watched through bars, a lion,
a wild man, a pink lady, music
that followed in strange waves,
and your father holding your hand.

Sometimes it happens the lion
or wild man, or the pink lady,
breaks loose, and the music descends
over your life and you drown—
that's what your father says, calmly,
beside you. You turn your face toward it,
and you know: sometimes it happens.

WATCHING A CANDLE

A candle went down its own long stair
slowly, slowly, to see for itself.
Itself was the nothing it found,
and went out. No one in the dark,
I watched it all night. I was
myself in the morning. A friend
in the mirror saw me and waved
my steady hand, and I watched it wave.

CHILD IN THE EVENING

Why does this house have no windows, Mother?
Windows weaken a wall, My Son.

Why is it low, with nothing around?
The world is too bright and distracting, My Son.

Where are the neighbors, the friends, all gone?
They followed the years. They do that, My Son.

But I have sworn never to forsake them—
this place is lonely. I belong with my friends.
It is all right. They may come in.
This house is for everyone.

MURDER BRIDGE

You look over the edge, down, down . . .
there's where the poor crazy mother threw
them, all three, her children she loved. They hurtled
and struck far there, once, then whirled
from rock to rock on into the rapid,
were found miles on, pieces their mother
had to see forever, the rest of her life.

It's quiet here. The rocks dream in the sun.
Our parents remembered the story. Our hands
gripped white on the railing. We felt the earth tilt.
We never thought the world was easy, as we
drove on. Luck—it takes luck and the sun
shining, and that mother recovered and crying
in our world saying, "Little ones, little ones."

SEEING AND PERCEIVING

You learn to like the scene that everything
in passing loans to you—a crooked tree
syncopated upward branch by pre-
established branch, its pattern suddening
as you study it; or a piece of string
forwarding itself, that straight knot so free
you puzzle slowly at its form (you see
intricate but fail at simple); or a wing,
the lost birds trailing home.
These random pieces begin to dance at night
or when you look away. You cling to them
for form, the only way that it will come
to the fallible: little bits of light
reflected by the sympathy of sight.

MAYBE

Maybe (it's a fear), maybe
someone decides. Maybe it takes
only one. Maybe the end begins.
Maybe it has begun.

It runs through the stages fast,
and they all respond well
and it's over. Then an explorer
comes.

What could they have done?
They could have tried harder.
They could have become meaner.
But maybe nothing—*it happened.*

The explorer turns over a stone.
Maybe those who sang
were the lucky ones.

HOW IT IS

It is war. They put us on a train and
say, "Go." A bell wakes up the engine
as we move along past the crowd,
and a child—one clear small gaze from all the town—
finds my face. I wave. For long I look
back. "I'm not a soldier," I want to say.
But the gaze is left behind. And I'm gone.

A LATE GUEST

I guess I thought it was music—that sound
at the party; they had the moon, that sort of old
light only the rich—or the desperate poor—
can clutch. I hid my shadow inside me
and stood by the door, realizing in a flood
that their terrace when I knocked would suddenly stop.

I knocked. In the long instant that followed
their house paled into glass and I was
a mirror they heard come into place
around them. It wasn't music. They froze.
All that they thought they had, they had to
give back in one glance when my shadow leaped.

Revelers, I'm sorry: I have to knock
in order to know if it really is music.

LATER

Sometimes, loping along, I almost find
that band of sorrow the wolves found. Long nights
they steal forth where moonlight follows their breath;
they bring their faces near and let the whining
begin: it strings puppy and wolf together.
That long pang across the horizon tells
how a hunter called Man will come. In the night by a fire
their guttural plan will blaze. A banner of woe,
the wolf cry goes in the wind, lifting their moan.

Now they are almost extinguished. Their tendered song
has melted into The North, where trees and stones
wait for our song, when we meet in the cold
with our faces near and begin our low whine
that means we are on the trail the wolves have gone.

IN A CORNER

Walls hold each other up when they meet;
a ceiling joins them: that corner you can
study, in jail or hospital or school.
I leaned in a corner once when someone
was dying, and I didn't care if the rest
of the walls went anywhere, or if the ceiling
or floor, or if anything—I didn't care.

Now if I'm traveling maybe a bad headache
sends me to lean in a corner. Each eye
has a wall. Father, Mother—they're gone,
and that person died, when I leaned before.
The corner never feels little enough,
and I roll my head for the world, for its need
and this wild, snuggling need and pain of my own.

WHY I SAY ADIOS

From their wide, still country words
descend, carrying their small, consistent
slant; and sometimes, usually
near the end, one of them hints a glimpse
of that silent country farther away.

Then with something like a wave
at the last, comes a word with a shimmer:
it spins into talk. People are looking
out—they belong elsewhere—, but the word
brings them in: they are surrounded by what
the word means. In their cloud they taste
slowly all that arrives when that word does.

There are these vistas behind all talk,
deep, temporary gulfs where the abode
for all passing things looms. We may
hurry past these; we may be jaunty
and skip along, subject, predicate, object;
but sometimes we let a proportion word in—
"So long," we say, "Vaya con dios,"
"God be with you," "Goodby!"—and the distance
beyond the stars deepens again.

REMEMBERING

When there was air, when you could
breathe any day if you liked, and if you
wanted to you could run, I used to
climb those hills back of town and
follow a gully so my eyes were at ground
level and could look out through grass as the stems
bent in their tensile way, and see snow
mountains follow along, the way distance goes.

Now I carry those days in a tiny box
wherever I go. I open the lid like this
and let the light glimpse and then glance away.
There is a sigh like my breath when I do this.
Some days I do this again and again.

PART THREE

REVELATIONS

Sending These Messages

Over these writings I bent my head.
Now you are considering them. If you
turn away I will look up: a bridge
that was there will be gone.
For the rest of your life I will stand here,
reaching across.

If these writings can bring a turn
or an echo that touches you—maybe
a face, a slant, a tune—you will stop
too and bend over them. When you
look up, your thought will reach
wherever I am.

I know it is strange. And there's no measure
for this. The only connection we make
is like a twinge when sometimes they change
the beat in music, and we sprawl with it
and hear another world for a minute
that is almost there.

A GLASS FACE IN THE RAIN

Sometime you'll walk all night. You'll
come where the sky bends down. You'll turn
aside at a fold in the earth and
be gone from the day.

When the sky turns light again
the land will stare blank for miles
at itself. You won't be there
to see any more.

Back where you lived, for those
who remember well, there will come
a glass face, invisible but still and real,
all night outside in the rain.

YELLOW CARS

Some of the cars are yellow, that go
by. Those you look at, so glimmering
when light glances at their passing. Think
of that hope: "Someone will
like me, maybe." The tan ones
don't care, the blue have made
a mistake, the white haven't tried.
But the yellow—you turn your head:
hope lasts a long time if you're happy.

TORQUE

One day all the people come out on the street
and look at each other. Something is at
their throats, or as if a big magnet has hummed
and surrounded them with lines in the air.

Face gazes at face and then
up at the sky—nothing. Backs
arch, arms tighten and pull
out like limbs of trees, trembling.

But there is nothing. And it passes away.
People relax and stand there. The sun
is the same. Down the street a car
revs as usual. Nothing. Nothing.

Suppose this happens. The world looks
tame, but might go wild, any time.

MY LIFE

In my cradle and then driving
my little car, I wave and listen.
(Meanwhile the Cossacks line up together
beyond the horizon, each of them like me,
but maybe older, but lost. But coming.)

Pretty soon I am running. It is
daylight pretty soon and then very bright
across fields by the road. Someone
begins calling. I think it is a person, but maybe
an animal, maybe a bird. I can't tell.

And now it is hard to remember what didn't happen—
did I hear thunder? I stop and look
at the others—does the lightning come
before or after? And even if I find out—
will my soul be happy, out here alone?

From over there in the trees a slant
glance comes, like my father's to find
my mother's, and this film we are in
spins backward, and then I am gone
and pretty soon there isn't any world.

A MESSAGE FROM SPACE

Everything that happens is the message:
you read an event and be one and wait,
like breasting a wave, all the while knowing
by living, though not knowing how to live.

Or workers build an antenna—a dish
aimed at stars—and they themselves are its message,
crawling in and out, being worlds that loom,
dot-dash, and sirens, and sustaining beams.

And sometimes no one is calling but we turn up
eye and ear—suddenly we fall into
sound before it begins, the breathing
so still it waits there under the breath—

And then the green of leaves calls out, hills
where they wait or turn, clouds in their frenzied
stillness unfolding their careful words:
"Everything counts. The message is the world."

REVELATION

When I came back to earth, it was my bike
threw me. I woke to day not real day—
some of the sunlight came like bottles piled
in a window frame. People were pictures with labels,
"Doctor," "intern," "aide." I remember a cookie
big as the sun that lasted as long as a glass of milk.

Some day your world won't last all day. You'll blink;
you'll fall to earth; and where the ocean was
will be that color *here* was before you came:
your head and what you hit will sound the same.

ON THE ROAD LAST NIGHT

On the road last night I heard the tires
accepting their rendezvous the way I would meet
the rest of the world, wherever it is,
wherever I am, one place then the next
always expected—"Hello, glad to meet you,"
"Goodby, so long." And then just the road.

AFTER ARGUING AGAINST THE
CONTENTION THAT ART MUST COME
FROM DISCONTENT

Whispering to each handhold, "I'll be back,"
I go up the cliff in the dark. One place
I loosen a rock and listen a long time
till it hits, faint in the gulf, but the rush
of the torrent almost drowns it out, and the wind—
I almost forgot the wind: it tears at your side
or it waits and then buffets; you sag outward. . . .

I remember they said it would be hard. I scramble
by luck into a little pocket out of
the wind and begin to beat on the stones
with my scratched numb hands, rocking back and forth
in silent laughter there in the dark—
"Made it again!" Oh how I love this climb!
—the whispering to stones, the drag, the weight
as your muscles crack and ease on, working
right. They are back there, discontent,
waiting to be driven forth. I pound
on the earth, riding the earth past the stars:
"Made it again! Made it again!"

A COURSE IN CREATIVE WRITING

They want a wilderness with a map—
but how about errors that give a new start?—
or leaves that are edging into the light?—
or the many places a road can't find?

Maybe there's a land where you have to sing
to explain anything: you blow a little whistle
just right and the next tree you meet is itself.
(And many a tree is not there yet.)

Things come toward you when you walk.
You go along singing a song that says
where you are going becomes its own
because you start. You blow a little whistle—

And a world begins under the map.

THINGS I LEARNED LAST WEEK

Ants, when they meet each other,
usually pass on the right.

Sometimes you can open a sticky
door with your elbow.

A man in Boston has dedicated himself
to telling about injustice.
For three thousand dollars he will
come to your town and tell you about it.

Schopenhauer was a pessimist but
he played the flute.

Yeats, Pound, and Eliot saw art as
growing from other art. They studied that.

If I ever die, I'd like it to be
in the evening. That way, I'll have
all the dark to go with me, and no one
will see how I begin to hobble along.

In The Pentagon one person's job is to
take pins out of towns, hills, and fields,
and then save the pins for later.

INCIDENT

They had this cloud they kept like a zeppelin
tethered to a smokestack, and you couldn't see it
but it sent out these strange little rays
and after a while you felt funny. They had this
man with a box. He pointed it at
the zeppelin and it said, "Jesus!" The man
hurried farther away and called out,
"Hear ye, hear ye!" Then they coaxed
the zeppelin down into the smokestack
and they said, "We won't do that any more."
For a long time the box kept shaking its head,
but it finally said, "Ok, forget it." But, quietly,
to us, it whispered, "Let's get out of here."

.

FICTION

We would get a map of our farm as big
as our farm, and unroll the heavy paper
over the fields, with encouraging things
written here and there—"tomatoes," "corn,"
"creek." Then in the morning we would
stick our heads through and sing, "Barn, be cleaned."
"Plow, turn over the south forty!"
But while our words were going out
on the paper, here would come rumpling
along under the map Old Barney,
just on the ground—he couldn't even
read—going out to slop the hogs.

OUR KIND

Our mother knew our worth—
not much. To her, success
was not being noticed at all.
"If we can stay out of jail,"
she said, "God will be proud of us."

"Not worth a row of pins,"
she said, when we looked at the album:
"Grandpa?—ridiculous."
Her hearing was bad, and that
was good: "None of us ever says much."

She sent us forth equipped
for our kind of world, a world of
our betters, in a nation so strong
its greatest claim is no boast,
its leaders telling us all, "Be proud"—

But over their shoulders, God and
our mother, signaling: "Ridiculous."

HANGING TOUGH

All right, I'll ask about home:—How is the grass
that lived all over the hills? Does the cottonwood
tree still dance by the road to town?
Has the river found that island it talked
about all night to the bridge? Do the houses
wait for the moon and offer their porches?

But the people I won't ask about. Their voices
lurk behind their doors, where they always were,
for me. As I turn away I'll say it again—
after their wars, after their various affairs,
their lives they'll just have to take care of all alone,
    for themselves.

LEARNING TO LIKE THE NEW SCHOOL

They brought me where it was bright and said,
"Be bright." I couldn't even see. They tried
again: "Look up." I tried but it
was all sad to me. They turned and went
away. And then it all came on
to be a world like this—you learn only
the one clear lesson, "How It Is":
the rain falls, the wind blows,
and you are just there, alone, as yourself.
The world is no test—"So you got here, fine,"
any new place says. And you say, "Yes, I'm here."

A CATECHISM

Who challenged my soldier mother?
  Nobody.
Who kept house for her and fended off the world?
  My father.
Who suffered most from her oppressions?
  My sister.
Who went out into the world to right its wrongs?
  My sister.
Who became bitter when the world didn't listen?
  My sister.
Who challenged my soldier sister?
  Nobody.
Who grew up and saw all this and recorded it and
kept wondering how to solve it but couldn't?
  Guess who.

SCHOOL DAYS

1

After the test they sent an expert
questioner to our school: "Who is this
kid Bohr?" When Bohr came in
he asked the expert, "Who are you?"
and for a long time they looked at each other,
and Bohr said, "Thanks, I thought so." Then
they talked about why the test was given.
Afterwards they shook hands, and Bohr walked
slowly away. He turned and called out, "You passed."

2

Enough sleet had pasted over the window
by three o'clock so we couldn't tell if it was dark—
and our pony would be out there in the little shed
waiting to take us home. Teacher banked the stove
with an extra log. That was the storm
of 1934. For two days we waited,
singing and praying, and I guess it worked,
even though the snow drifted over the roof.
But the pony was dead when they dug us out.

3

At a tiny desk inside my desk, a doll
bends over a book. In the book is a feather
found at the beach, from a dead gull.
While Miss Leonard reads "The Highwayman,"
I bend over my book and cry,
and fly all alone through the night
toward being the person I am.

WE INTERRUPT TO BRING YOU

It will be coming toward Earth, and
a cameraman who happens to be on Mt. Palomar or
somewhere will catch it, live, for the news,
and I'll be going to the bathroom or something
and miss it; or maybe I'm out raking leaves
in the yard, or it's one of those days I'm home
with flu, and being feverish I doze, but it's
all right to skip work because I'm really
sick, a little bit; anyway, it's the greatest
scene ever, and I don't see it—they call
an alert, and everybody panics; it's coming
like mad, and everybody hightails out—
they clear New York, and all the people rush
into shelters or those new domes on the ocean
floor, and everybody's gone, and the domes
collapse, and I'm the only one left.

And it's still coming on toward Earth, but
at the last minute it misses, and I
come back from the bathroom or from raking,
or just wake up, and the channels are funny;
I switch around and find one still going—it's
on automatic pilot or something—and it just
keeps going back and back through old commercials
and Saturday morning horrors, and people are all
dead, or gone anyway, but the world is
saved and I'm watching this one dim channel,
thinking: it's still a good day even though
I can't get Perry Mason—the leaves
are all raked, and I'm not very sick, really.

MY MOTHER WAS A SOLDIER

If no one moved on order, she would kill—
that's what the gun meant, soldier. No one
told you? Her eye went down the barrel; her hand
held still; gunpowder paid all that it owed
at once. No need to count the dead.

Hunting, she dragged the bait till nightfall, then
hung it in a tree and waited. Time
was working for her, and the quiet. What a world
it is, for thinkers! Contact would come, and
the wildest foe fall fastest, Mother said.

Tapping on my wrist, she talked: "Patience
is the doctor; it says try; it says
they think we're nice, we quiet ones, we die
so well: that's how we win, imagining things
before they happen." "No harm in being quiet,"

My mother said: "that's the sound that finally wins."

ANTICIPATING

Keeping your word is like putting a bell into
a future memory, to wait there. You hold
that stilled bell hidden, but you know
where the sound will be, deep and slow,
ready to toll all day, all night, miles around.
Others may change their word. They can pile rocks
on it. They back away. They dance on the stones.
But the bell waits in its crypt. And it slowly moves.

WHEN YOU GO ANYWHERE

This passport your face (not you
officially, your picture, but the face
used to make the passport) offers
everyone its witness: "This is me."

It feels like only a picture, a passport
forced upon you. Somewhere this oval,
sudden and lasting, appeared. It happened
that you were behind it, like it or not.

You present it—your passport, your face—
wherever you go. It says, "A little country,"
it says, "Allow this observer
quiet passage," it says, "Ordinary," it says, "Please."

PART FOUR

TROUBLESHOOTING

Now wait—

*If you close this book, one page
will touch the page across, a word
will touch another word.*

*Just think that kiss across
the page, how clenched it is—
and all we say is, and deep,*

*What you say, and I say, X-ray remarks
jumbled at once. We don't mean things
just one by one, but give and take,*

*Your eyes, my lips, your ears, my
heart. This book takes them,
to press, to keep.*

Now start.

ONCE IN THE 40'S

We were alone one night on a long
road in Montana. This was in winter, a big
night, far to the stars. We had hitched,
my wife and I, and left our ride at
a crossing to go on. Tired and cold—but
brave—we trudged along. This, we said,
was our life, watched over, allowed to go
where we wanted. We said we'd come back some time
when we got rich. We'd leave the others and find
a night like this, whatever we had to give,
and no matter how far, to be so happy again.

AROUND YOU, YOUR HOUSE

I give you the rain, its long hollow
room all the way down to the streetlight
yellow under midnight. I give you the sound
you can hear when drops are talking to
themselves while you are staring from a window.
I give you a letter. You can fold it again
and carry it when you walk back to the fire
where you stand for a while. I give you the poker
for stirring what burns, one page at a time.
The last flames up the draft and out
into the night, and I give you the rain.

A CAMEO OF YOUR MOTHER

What the blind have for their light
is more than light. Remembering
precedes the things remembered. You put
your hand out through immediate space—
that face rewarded by forever
waits inside your life, a touch
of light survived in amethyst.

RUBY WAS HER NAME

My mother, who opened my eyes, who
brought me into the terrible world,
was guilty. Her look apologized:
she knew what anyone said was true about us
but therefore unfair. How could they blame us
for doing the things we were set to do?

Never heroic, never a model
for us, or for anyone, she cowered
and looked from the corner of her eye—
"Et tu?" And it always meant we were
with her, alas. No one else
could find the center of the world.

She found the truth like a victim; it hit
her again and again, and she always cried out.
At the end she turned to me, helplessly
honest still: "Oh, Bill, I'm afraid,"
and the whole of her life went back to her heart,
from me in a look for the look she gave.

AT THE FALLS: A BIRTHDAY PICTURE

A few leaves flutter still, even on the maple,
in the picture. Over your shoulder another
person waits. If I gaze long enough
you move past now and carry us all
down the corridor where the eyes are,
and we find everything changed. I could be sorry,
but even to put out my hand would hurt more.
From your side of the picture you can watch foam
electing its moment of plunge and then—gone.
You stand on the brink and wait. You can be
still. You can smile. I'm the one with the fears.

It always was cold, those years.

LETTING YOU GO

Day brings what is going to be. Trees—
wherever they are—begin to stand.
I have a crossing to do today
onward through this shadowy land.

How still earth stayed that night at first
when you didn't breathe. I couldn't believe
how carefully moonlight came. It was
like the time by my mother's grave.

Today I am going on. In former times
when you were back there, then
I tried to hold the moon and sun.
Now when they ask me who you were—

I remember, but remember my promise.
And I say, "No one."

TROUBLESHOOTING

On still days when country telephone
wires go south, go home, go quietly away into
the woods, a certain little brown bird appears,
hopping and flying by starts, following the line,
trying out each pole.
My father and I, troubleshooting for the telephone
company back then, used to see that same bird
along old roads, and it led us to farms
we always thought about owning some day.

When I see that bird now I see my father
tilt his hat and flip the pliers confidently
into the toolbox; the noise of my life, and all
the buffeting from those who judge and pass by,
dwindle off and sink into the silence,
and the little brown bird steadfastly wanders on
pulling what counts wherever it goes.

A LETTER NOT TO DELIVER

Why should it be anguish (but anguish
it is) accepting the gift you are?
I see your eyes: listen—I care
what happens, and why it happens.
And that there isn't anything at the end.

I don't want you to know. I hope
you search. You can wonder. I hope
the buffeting around us pleases you—
it is all there is. And because I like
your face, when you turn toward me
I hear a long silence.

HAVING THE RIGHT NAME

It is like a color inside your head that
tells who you really are, or like that air
moving through trees whispering to you at night.

People will want to be with you
on a list, beside your name. They will be glad
they are themselves, but able to reach across.

Sometimes you'll forget, but a shadow leans
from behind a hill over your life
where someone hides calling your name aloud.

So you needn't care who walks the fields
lost in the snow all night: any track
spells the needed word at dawn when you look out.

A DAY TO REMEMBER

I'm standing at Lakeside Drive with my bike.
It is dusk. I didn't think anybody would care
if I'm lonely, a bicycle in traffic, young
and hence guilty, some kind of oddity nobody
would have. And here came this wind. Sometimes
even snow is *for* you somehow, and this was.
I belonged. It was 1935, the day
I became saved and a citizen of the world.

REMEMBERING BROTHER BOB

Tell me, you years I had for my life,
tell me a day, that day it snowed
and I played hockey in the cold.
Bob was seven, then, and I was twelve,
and strong. The sun went down. I turned
and Bob was crying on the shore.

Do I remember kindness? Did I
shield my brother, comfort him?
Tell me, you years I had for my life.

Yes, I carried him. I took
him home. But I complained. I see
the darkness, it comes near: and Bob,
who is gone now, and the other kids.
I am the zero in the scene:
"You said you would be brave," I chided
him. "I'll not take you again."
Years, I look at the white across
this page, and think: I never did.

PLACES WITH MEANING

Say it's a picnic on the Fourth of July
and all of those usual at the end of day are there.
While they look at each other they become old,
and from the dark wood of evening a heron
rows forward across the path of sky left
in the west, through the still air.

All of my life I have noticed these appropriate landscapes
where events find their equivalent forms: oftentimes
I see trees hunching their shoulders, leaning toward me,
because in the past I have neglected what I should have done;
or a dog hurries forward to lick some hands, and all
at once I see how frightening: they are mine.

There are people who always belong wherever Earth brings
them and gives them over to the practices of the wind;
more slowly, but caught in the same pressure, the rest of us
too, by the end of our days, learn to lean forward
out of our lives to find that what passes has molded
everything we touch or see, outside or in.

CONFESSOR

The girl hiding in the hall on the ferry
from Alaska, the old man who kept his face
in shadow, that matron shuddering over
the market basket in the parking lot—
scores of these follow me into my dreams,
and I can't tell more because I promised.

I carry their burden. When I go down
the street my memory is a vault that no one
need see opened. I am their plain
unmarked envelope that passes through the world.
People tell me what they don't want to carry
alone. They have felt singled out by some
blow: not always at fault but still
ashamed for a human involvement, they want
someone else to know, to bear with them
and not blame. I am their stranger and will pass
out of their life. . . .

All right. I listen. My life sinks a little
farther, for the pity; from now on I know it
with them. We'll take a stand, wherever the end is.
We go forward by this quiet sharing,
they one way, I another. I am their promise:
no one else is going to know.

A SCENE

Grandpa gives me a candy watch,
which I slowly eat, slowly peeling
its paper face. Along our street
a slow wind uncurls the world,
widens gutters, takes down trees
for the new houses. Every house, even
the doctor's, dissolves for history.
Some assessor colder than winter takes
down the names. I balance on the curb
and from three feet high look up
at Grandpa to take his hand.
Through the slow wind, we face toward you,
and stand.

WITH NEIGHBORS ONE AFTERNOON

Someone said, stirring their tea, "I would
come home any time just for this,
to look out the clear backyard air
and then into the cup."

You could see the tiniest pattern of bark on the trees
and every slight angle of color change
in the sunshine—millions of miles of gold light
lavished on people like us.

You could put out your hand and feel the rush of years
rounding your life into these days of ours.
From somewhere a leaf came gliding slowly down
and rested on the lawn.

Remember that scene?—inside it you folded the last
of your jealousy and hate, and all those deeds so hard
to forget. Absolution: swish!—you took
the past into your mouth,

And swallowed it, warm, thin, bitter, and good.

ABSENCES

Once when the waves were talking one said
"I'll never be back." And then the rest
ran on toward shore, but that one went forth
so far it's never been seen again.

When you walk along sometimes, you think
of that absent wave—and of all that doesn't
exist any more, things of the other
years. "They'll never be back," you say.

You stop and look out. It's already tomorrow
somewhere, and someone like you is walking;
a wave is beginning to speak, and the rest
shrug and go on. You stand and care.

Much has never existed, you know.
You think of things to say. The waves
come in. Wherever you walk you see
a place for that wave. But it isn't there.

PART FIVE

THE COLOR THAT
REALLY IS

A Tentative Welcome to Readers

It is my hope that those who blame
these tentatives may find some other
reading and be supremely matched
by pieces worthy of them. I offer
these I've found—no claims except
their being mine. A glance may serve—do these
belong inside your life? My life,
Reader, encountered these trancelike
events that I've turned into things to tell.
If you like them, fine. If not, farewell.

THE COLOR THAT REALLY IS

The color that really is comes over a desert
after the sun goes down: blue, lavender,
purple. . . . What if you saw all this in the day?
And the sun itself, those rays our eyes jump through
on their way to light, what swords come out of that globe
and slice—life, death, disguise—through space!

Once I was going along and met in Reno
by a table a woman with a terrible face: I saw it
under a lamp that revealed what a desert was
if you lived there the way it is. She had found
what was left in her life after the sun went down.

Since then I pause every day to bow my head
and know, as well as I can, the light, and behind
that light the other glow that waits to shine
for those who survive past noon and by luck are saved
for a while from those rays that could find anyone any time.

JOURNEY

Through many doors it's been—through
that first into light, afraid, crying
for fear, for air, no going back.
Then other doors: the one where shadows
waited like night, the one nobody
opened when I knocked, and the one where somebody
did. (It was over a cliff and I fell.)

One time there wasn't any door; I turned to look
where I had been—only that? Only
those meaningless windows leading down one
by one to the faint small beginning?

Past the middle of life, and nothing
done—but a voice came on: "I am
the door," someone said. I closed my eyes;
whatever I touched led on.

FRIENDS, FAREWELL

After the chores are done I tune
and strum. Nobody hears, nobody cares,
and the stars go on.

Now that I've told you this, maybe
I've been all wrong—so faint a life,
and so little done.

But I want you all to be easy after
I'm gone: nobody hear, nobody care,
and the stars go on.

IF I COULD BE LIKE
WALLACE STEVENS

The octopus would be my model—
it wants to understand; it prowls
the rocks a hundred ways and holds
its head aloof but not ignoring.
All its fingers value what
they find. "I'd rather know," they say,
"I'd rather slime along than be heroic."

My pride would be to find out; I'd
bow to see, play the fool,
ask, beg, retreat like a wave—
but somewhere deep I'd hold the pearl,
never tell. "Mr. Charley,"
I'd say, "talk some more. Boast again."
And I'd play the banjo and sing.

YELLOW FLOWERS

While I was dying I saw a flower
by the road—yellow, with a rough
green stem. It had what I always
admire—patience, and the one great
virtue, being only itself. I was lying
where the wreck had thrown me, and I heard my pulse
telling me, "Come back, come back, come back."

I remembered a candle. It was at the end
of a row in church. Wind made it flicker.
It almost went out, but came back when left
alone. World with your flower, your candle:—
we flicker and bend; we hear wheels
on the road—any sight, any sound—that music
the soul takes and makes it its own.

SALVAGED PARTS

Fire took the house. Black bricks
tell how it went. Wild roses
try to say it never happened.

A rock my foot pushed falls
for years down the cellar stairs. . . .
No thanks, no home again for me—

Mine burned before it burned.
A rose pretends, but I always knew:
a rose pretends, a rock tells how it is.

SURVIVOR

Remember that party we had, the one
we all said we'd always remember?
No, not last year—longer ago.
I was thinking of making a custom of going
back there and saying the names. I'd stand
under the streetlight; I'd imagine the rain
that hollowed our town in an arch of silver.
Joyce would be there, and the shadows around
her face; a call down the street, and it would
be all the rest at once. I would fall:
rising out of my head like moths
in the autumn dusk, everything we promised
each other would whirl away. Every
year I would do this, because I might
forget sometime and we all be gone,
who said that night we'd always remain.

ONE TIME

When evening had flowed between houses
and paused on the schoolground, I met
Hilary's blind little sister following
the gray smooth railing still warm from the sun
with her hand; and she stood by the edge
holding her face upward waiting
while the last light found her cheek
and her hair, and then on over the trees.

You could hear the great sprinkler arm
of water find and then leave the pavement,
and pigeons telling each other their dreams
or the dreams they would have. We were
deep in the well of shadow by then, and I
held out my hand, saying, "Tina, it's me—
Hilary says I should tell you it's dark,
and, oh, Tina, it is. Together now—"

And I reached, our hands touched,
and we found our way home.

LITTLE NIGHT STORIES

There was a certain flake. For miles it
tumbled along becoming its real self
lost in its crystal story—crystals
never forsake whatever they first elect.
And so it came to its place, frail
as a piece of lace dipped in pretty
words: "Honor," "Courage," "Hope."

Listen—such words make up the self—
unravel them and it's gone, not even
a thread is left. Even "Cowardice" will help—
it's a human trait in the cold of the universe,
and we have to embrace all we are, in this,
our story: a flake, a flake, a flake.

RECEIVER

Listening late at parties, hearing
the quiet ones, dead keys on the piano
lifting their deep report, how they
used to have names to drop all evening
before those rooms went dark—

Such times I've gone out alone, quiet
in the woods, and waited by a little fire:
that's when the night-room comes, hovering
near, hollowed out by an owl,
and I in the center to hear—

Or out along water, to put in my hand
under the starlight: before the shine,
a little ripple begins, and a fragile
white web floats up, a message for someone
like me, far, there on the shore.

FROM HALLMARK OR SOMEWHERE

Think now of a mountain—say, that one
south of Medicine Bow. Does it make
any difference at all, what you are thinking?
"None at all," do you say? "None to that mountain"?
Only one person in the world thinking of
a certain place, and it means nothing? Nothing?

If someone is thinking of you—no difference
to you if you don't know it? None?
Then telling you so is the difference? That's all?
Someone sends you this card, no matter
the reason. You look out over some trees.
You tap on the card and ponder. Strange—
you care whether the card is true,
even when it just says, "I am thinking of you."

MUCH HAVE I TRAVELED

When we heard it like the ocean
and climbed farther to listen
down there in our cave,
it was only our blood
rushing to save us,
a new tide every second
rustling along a shore
deep into gulf mountains
glimpsed that first dark day
from our peak in Darien.

Closer and closer to
our own, our own,
we curled from winters
the world heaped on us,
and "Proclaim!" the heart said
back and forth by its beating
without any order or
promises at all, no one
to cheer it its whole
life long.

It gave us this mandala
both of us found:
the sun through clouds, and
earth hiding in mist,
a face at a time that
comes floating toward us
when we try to be good.
There is no other tide
so strong as this tide
in the silence of the world.

ONCE IN A DREAM

Once after we hid from each other you passed
staring through what had been me—I beckoned
but could not call. Where I stood was numb.
I was in glass it seemed, and gone
from your world; yet you were in mine, but more:
with a yearning too strong for me to withstand,
when you went by, I leaned.

Such passing in after times may be—
you and I burning like candles, but locked
each in a separate room, more than
ever alive but never again to touch,
even in a place called home.

THE LATE FLIGHT

Home from far, moon on the wing,
riding in airplane language, our shadow
afraid over the snow, voices
in the plane around us—I thought in a great
sweep of hope: "Maybe this will all be
saved." Engines tiptoed their monster
caverns; people around me breathed.

I knew the engines would win, but power
can't keep a quicksilver self in check:
from beyond the stars I came back toward now,
where I live. There was a voice that said
everything the silence hears; and I heard it
while watching the moon ride beside me,
saying itself, saying light, saying,
"It's hard." "I'm alone." "Where are the years?"

WHAT EVER HAPPENED TO
THE BEATS?

On that street in San Francisco
in a room behind the temple
where a hand was always clapping,
it has stopped to listen
for the sound of the other hand.

Many will fall again where these
chosen fell: they ran to meet what
came, a war one generation, peace and
its drugs the next. Veterans now,
they hobble on, still shouting, "Now!"

On the corner a church has a sign:
The hardest war to fight
is the one you don't know you're in,
the one it takes quiet to find.

WHAT I'LL SEE THAT AFTERNOON

The young man who has to look
sideways through his glasses to see.
The lady with the little dog. (I'll put
down my pack.) A car jerking and
popping with its engine cold. Four bicycles
in line unreeling their shadows. (I'll
slowly stand up.) Down by the corner
someone beginning to scream. A brick
wall that breaks halfway across. (With a
whirl of my head I'll see it all tilt.)
The girl with the face. A piece of paper
caught in that corner tree.
(Everything stops,
and I am reaching out for everything.)

PEGLEG LOOKOUT

Those days, having the morning clouds, and with no one
around, it was quiet on the lookout.
For breakfast I ate animal crackers
and milk in a blue bowl marked
"World's Fair, 1939." Some of the figures
looked like my mother. I saved those till last.
Then I sat on the deck reading "War
and Peace," "The Magic Mountain," "David
Copperfield"—the big ones I'd brought. Four times
an hour I paced the catwalk to look
for smokes—nothing, the miles of pine tops
and then Mount Shasta. Those days I ate
the whole world, lined up my books and animals,
slowly erased all the trials and insults
the times had brought. I balanced my life
there a whole year. One day I washed
the blue bowl the last time and came down again.

YUCCA FLOWERS

In the hills today if you bow
you can feel the mild yellow
report of yucca flowers, those
quiet guns the air puffs forth
when people are gone.

You can feel how the quail
return, if you bow in the hills
today—feathers and grass, a wave
of the earth, and feet creating
little stories in dust on the old paths.

And here is the last: no one
is going to return; there will be
gaps in the air, places like flowers
no one can see. Today you can feel
them still, if you bow in the hills.

FROM OUR BALLOON OVER
THE PROVINCES

From our balloon floating early
mornings we heard from sleeping
farms when the roosters pierced
quiet shells, re-echoing
how lonely their lives had been
cooped up in an egg.

And roads in the sandhills went off
past ponds and ended
at fields. In the summer
it was water and bees made
the air always alive, and in
the winter, snow.

Those things that we met come back
now, always reminding that
the world out there—not caring who
we are—reaches us millions of ways:
little fireflies quiet as truth
climbing their invisible trellis of dark.

INDEX OF TITLES

Absences   96
A Cameo of Your Mother   83
A Catechism   72
A Child's Face in a Small Town   42
Acoma Mesa   36
A Course in Creative Writing   65
A Day to Remember   90
After Arguing Against the Contention That Art
    Must Come from Discontent   64
A Glass Face in the Rain   57
A Glimpse in the Crowd   38
A Journey   100
A Late Guest   49
A Letter Not to Deliver   88
A Message from Space   61
An Event at Big Eddy   28
An Old Pickerel in Walden Pond   34
Anticipating   76
Around You, Your House   82
A Scene   94
A Tentative Welcome to Readers   97
A Touch on Your Sleeve   20
At the Falls: A Birthday Picture   85
Child in the Evening   44
Class Reunion   40
Confessor   93
Dark Wind   37
Fiction   68

Finding Out   35
Friends   16
Friends: A Recognition   39
Friends, Farewell   101
From Hallmark or Somewhere   109
From Our Balloon over the Provinces   117
Glimpses   21
Hanging Tough   70
Having the Right Name   89
How It Began   13
How It Is   48
How to Get Back   29
If I Could Be Like Wallace Stevens   102
In a Corner   51
Incident   67
Knowing   18
Later   50
Learning to Like the New School   71
Letting You Go   86
Little Night Stories   107
Looking Across the River   22
Maybe   47
Much Have I Traveled   110
Murder Bridge   45
My Life   60
My Mother Was a Soldier   75
Not Very Loud   25
Now wait—   79
Once in a Dream   111
Once in the 40's   81
One Time   106
On the Road Last Night   63
Our Cave   24
Our Kind   69
Passing a Pile of Stones   27
Pegleg Lookout   115
Places with Meaning   92
Receiver   108
· 120 ·

Remembering 53
Remembering Brother Bob 91
Revelation 62
Rover 17
Ruby Was Her Name 84
Sabbath 41
Salvaged Parts 104
School Days 73
Seeing and Perceiving 46
Sending These Messages 55
Smoke Signals—a dedication 11
Some Night Again 30
Survivor 105
The Color That Really Is 99
The Late Flight 112
There Is Blindness 33
They Say 19
Things I Learned Last Week 66
Things That Come 31
Torque 59
Troubleshooting 87
Tuned in Late One Night 15
Watching a Candle 43
We Interrupt to Bring You 74
What Ever Happened to the Beats? 113
What I'll See That Afternoon 114
When You Go Anywhere 77
Why I Say Adios 52
Why We Need Fantasy 26
With Neighbors One Afternoon 95
Yellow Cars 58
Yellow Flowers 103
Yucca Flowers 116

INDEX OF FIRST LINES

A candle went down its own long stair   43
A few leaves flutter still, even on the maple,   85
After it came down from the mountains   31
After the chores are done I tune   101
After the test they sent an expert   73
A light—it's only the sun—has broken   41
All right, I'll ask about home:—How is the grass   70
Ants, when they meet each other,   66
A parachute catches and suddenly you know   38
A shadow hides in every stone.   27
Because it was good, we were afraid.   24
By believing, you can get there—that edge   29
Consider the slow descent   20
Day brings what is going to be. Trees—   86
Everything that happens is the message: 61
Fire took the house. Black bricks   104
From our balloon floating early   117
From their wide, still country words   52
Grandpa gives me a candy watch,   94
Home from far, moon on the wing,   112
How far friends are! They forget you,   16
If no one moved on order, she would kill—   75
If you close this book, one page   79
I give you the rain, its long hollow   82
I guess I thought it was music—that sound   49
I'm standing at Lakeside Drive with my bike.   90
In my cradle and then driving   60
In the hills today if you bow   116

It came silent in my thought   39
It is like a color inside your head that   89
It is my hope that those who blame   97
It is war. They put us on a train and   48
It's a sensational story   26
It will be coming toward Earth, and   74
Jean, who no longer is, was   37
Keeping your word is like putting a bell into   76
Listening late at parties, hearing   108
Listen—this is a faint station   15
Maybe (it's a fear), maybe   47
My mother, who opened my eyes, who   84
No, not dark. Even at night a glow from a shaft   35
Now and then in some sound you discover   19
Now is the time of the moths that come   25
Once after we hid from each other you passed   111
Once when the waves were talking one said   96
One day all the people come out on the street   59
One time when the wind blows it is years   21
One winter—open, I remember it was—   34
On still days when country telephone   87
On that street in San Francisco   113
On the road last night I heard the tires   63
Our mother knew our worth—   69
Over these writings I bent my head.   55
Remember that party we had, the one   105
Say it's a picnic on the Fourth of July   92
She came out of the field—low   17
Some of the cars are yellow, that go   58
Someone said, stirring their tea, "I would   95
Sometimes it happens a storm   42
Sometimes, loping along, I almost find   50
Sometime you'll walk all night. You'll   57
Surrounded by air, we live where   36
Tell me, you years I had for my life,   91
The color that really is comes over a desert   99
The girl hiding in the hall on the ferry   93
The octopus would be my model—   102

There are people on a parallel way. We do not   11
There is blindness; there is   33
There was a certain flake. For miles it   107
The whole weight of the river   28
They brought me where it was bright and said,   71
They had this cloud they kept like a zeppelin   67
The young man who has to look   114
They struggled their legs and blindly loved, those puppies   13
They want a wilderness with a map—   65
Think now of a mountain—say, that one   109
This passport your face (not you   77
Those days, having the morning clouds, and with no one   115
Through many doors it's been—through   100
To know the other world you turn   18
Walls hold each other up when they meet;   51
We were alone one night on a long   81
We were driving the river road.   22
We would get a map of our farm as big   68
What the blind have for their light   83
When evening had flowed between houses   106
When I came back to earth, it was my bike   62
When there was air, when you could   53
When the world vanishes, I will come back   30
When we heard it like the ocean   110
Where others ran I run my hand   40
While I was dying I saw a flower   103
Whispering to each handhold, "I'll be back,"   64
Who challenged my soldier mother?   72
Why does this house have no windows, Mother?   44
Why should it be anguish (but anguish   88
You learn to like the scene that everything   46
You look over the edge, down, down . . .—   45

COPYRIGHT ACKNOWLEDGMENTS

Grateful acknowledgment for permission to reprint is made to the following publications in which these poems first appeared.

Abraxas: Why We Need Fantasy. First published in *Abraxas* 21-22, © 1980 by Abraxas Press, Inc.
The American Poetry Review: Glimpses
The American Soldier: Things I Learned Last Week
The Ark 14 . . . For Rexroth: Survivor
Asphodel: Now Wait
Beyond Baroque: Having the Right Name
Black Warrior Review: Child in the Evening, Troubleshooting
Blair & Ketchum's *Country Journal*: A Touch on Your Sleeve
Blue Beech: A Child's Face in a Small Town, Places with Meaning
Canto: Learning to Like the New School
Carolina Quarterly: Letting You Go
CEA Critic: Class Reunion
The Chariton Review: My Mother Was a Soldier, Once in the 40's, A Scene
Chicago Review: Our Cave, An Old Pickerel in Walden Pond
The Chowder Review: A Journey
The Christian Science Monitor: One Time, Rover, Smoke Signals
Cimarron Review: Passing a Pile of Stones. First appeared in *Cimarron Review*; reprinted with the permission of The Board of Regents for Oklahoma State University, holders of the copyright.
Columbia—A Magazine of Poetry and Prose: How It Is
Conjunctions: Friends
Cornfield Review: From Hallmark or Somewhere
Crazy Horse: The Color That Really Is
The Deerfield Press: Tuned in Late One Night
Ellipsis: A Course in Creative Writing
Field: Absence, Maybe, Murder Bridge, Revelation, School Days, Yellow Cars
The Hampden-Sidney Poetry Review: How It Began, Our Kind
Harpoon: The Late Flight
Harvard Magazine: A Cameo of Your Mother, Knowing, Sabbath
Helix: Friends: A Recognition

Inquiry: A Day to Remember
The Iowa Review: Remembering Brother Bob
Kansas Quarterly: Fiction
Michigan Quarterly Review: In a Corner, Remembering
Modern Poetry Studies: Much Have I Traveled, What Ever Happened to the Beats?
The Nation: Acoma Mesa, Little Night Stories, Not Very Loud, Watching a Candle. Copyright 1977, 1979, *Nation* magazine, The Nation Associates, Inc.
National Forum: A Glimpse in the Crowd. Reprinted by permission from *National Forum: The Phi Kappa Phi Journal*, Vol. LIX, No. 2 (Spring, 1979), p. 48.
The New Yorker: An Event at Big Eddy, Yucca Flowers
Nimrod: At the Falls: A Birthday Picture
Northeastern University: A Late Guest
Pacific Northwest Review of Books: Finding Out
Paintbrush: My Life
The Paris Review: Ruby Was Her Name
Pequod: A Message from Space
Plainsong: Around You, Your House, A Catechism, Confessor, Friends, Farewell, A Letter Not to Deliver
Poetry: Looking Across the River, Sending These Messages, A Tentative Welcome to Readers, With Neighbors One Afternoon
Poetry Miscellany: Yellow Flowers
Practices of the Wind: Dark Wind, From Our Balloon over the Provinces, Why I Say Adios
Quest: Hanging Tough, Receiver, We Interrupt to Bring You
River Styx: A Glass Face in the Rain. First published in *River Styx 5*, 1979.
Rolling Stone: When You Go Anywhere
San Jose Studies: On the Road Last Night, What I'll See That Afternoon
Sceptre Press: How to Get Back, They Say
Slow Loris Press: Incident, Torque
South and West: Seeing and Perceiving
Spectrum: Once in a Dream
Tendril: After Arguing Against the Contention That Art Must Come from Discontent
Three Rivers Poetry Journal: Salvaged Parts, There Is Blindness. First appeared in *Three Rivers Poetry Journal*, copyright © 1977 by Three Rivers Press.
Three Sisters: Anticipating
Tinderbox: Some Night Again
Two Pears Press: Things That Come
The Virginia Quarterly Review: Pegleg Lookout
Wallace Stevens Journal: If I Could Be Like Wallace Stevens
Yankee: Later (published with the title "Anticipating")